THE RACE TO SPACE

An Introduction of Space to Children

Jvalin Tejpal

DREAMLAND

Published in 2007 by
DREAMLAND PUBLICATIONS
J-128, Kirti Nagar, New Delhi - 110 015 (India)
Tel : 011-2510 6050, Fax : 011-2543 8283
Copyright © 2007 Dreamland Publications
All rights reserved. No part of this book should be reproduced,
stored in a retrieval system or transmitted in any form or by any
means — electronic, mechanical, photocopying, recording or
otherwise —without the prior permission of
Dreamland Publications.

ISBN 81-7301-990-8

Printed at:
D. N. Offset Press

Illustrations by:
Harvinder Mankkar

Dedicated
To
The loving memory of my Grandfather

Acknowledgments

The writing of any book is the most difficult task to do and the same thing applies to me as well. Last one year and a half have been pretty tough to my family. None in the family was happy with the rigours of work that I was undertaking. I think my mother was affected the most, as, in her opinion, I was too young to undertake this task.

However, I am thankful to her for providing me emotional support and also for bearing with me for breaching house-discipline in eating, sleeping, socializing etc. which she, otherwise, enforces very strictly. My father has been of great help in going through the manuscript and giving me very constructive suggestions. He has been a pillar of strength for me and also a role-model. In fact, without the love and encouragement of my parents and my little sister 'Karnica', this book might not have come into existence.

I take this opportunity to thank (Dr.) Mrs.Shyama Chona, Principal D.P.S. R.K. Puram who has been always encouraging students like me and is a role-model to all the youngsters. She has been a big mental support throughout this venture. Last but not the least, I am overwhelmed by the constant support, I received from my Librarian in providing me books for a longer period than allowed. The Librarian's generous help has really improved quality of this work, as I got a lot of more references than what were, otherwise, available to me.

I am also thankful to Gaurima Yadav for her valuable suggestions and taking pains in going through the script of this book. I also acknowledge the support given by Mr. Suresh for correcting the typographical errors. Every effort has been made to trace the copyright holders and I apologize in advance for any unintentional omissions.

In the end, I am profoundly grateful to the Dreamland Publications for their gracious support in publishing this book.

CONTENTS

Solar System

Introduction & Composition of Solar System 5
Mercury 7
Hubble Space Telescope (HST) 9
Venus 10
Earth 11
Moon 13
Mars 14
Jupiter 16
Galileo 18
Saturn 19
Uranus 20
Neptune 21
Dwarf Planets 22

The Space Odyssey

Space Odyssey 26
Getting in Space 27
Breaking the Gravity Barrier & Life in Space 28
The Early Astronauts 29

Space-Your Work-Station

The Work-Station in Space 30
Types of Food & Keeping Fit 31
Take a Bath & Sleeping in Space 32
Experiments in Space & Space Walk 33

Space-Station

Space Excursion 35
International Space Station & Mir Space Station 36
Our Mission to the Moon & the Mars 37
Future Space Planes 39

India in Space

India in the World 41
India on the Moon 42
Satellites of India 43

Space-Records

Space Records of Solar System & Stars 46

Astronomy Chronology 57
Cosmology 64

Solar System

INTRODUCTION

Each one of us grows up gazing at the stars in the sky. There are innumerable anecdotes and myths surrounding these stars. Grandparents at some stage or the other tell us beautiful stories about the rising and the falling stars and so on. Our concept of God, Heaven and Hell, up in the sky gets developed through such tales. Similarly life being there up in the sky and also beneath the Earth must have been heard by all of us at some stage of our growing up process. Who can forget the legendary king *Ravana* of *Ramayana* fame who was so powerful as to rule *Dharti* (Earth), *Aakash* (Sky) and *Patal* (Under the Earth).

Why is it that, there is complete darkness in the night on some days whereas it is quite bright on some other nights? Why does the Moon keep on changing its shape everyday? Answers to all these myths, observations and facts will be found on the subsequent pages in this book. The reference to the *Ramayana* given above shows that even when history was not dated, people had some concept of life beyond the Earth. Since time immemorial human beings have been striving to understand the secrets of space and whatever knowledge we have today is an accumulation of our past knowledge. Before, I take you to this romantic journey of Human endeavour, it would be in the fitness of things that we briefly understand our neighbours in the Solar System. This would come handy to us while we take our seat in the Spacecraft and fasten our seatbelt for a wonderful experience about the space travel.

COMPOSITION OF THE SOLAR SYSTEM

The Earth is a part of our Solar system and the only planet on which life is known to exist. It is a unique planet.

Traditionally, the solar system has been divided into **planets** (the big bodies orbiting the Sun), their **Satellites** (a.k.a. moons, variously sized objects orbiting the planets), **asteroids** (small dense objects orbiting the Sun) and **comets** (small icy objects with highly eccentric orbits).

Unfortunately, the solar system has been found to be more complicated than this has been considered.

The Solar system consists of Sun, the eight official planets(Mercury, Venus, Earth, Mars, Jupiter, Saturn, Uranus and Neptune), at least four **"dwarf planet"** (*Pluto, Xena, Ceres* and *Charon*), more than 163 satellites of the planets, a large number of small bodies (the comets and asteroids), and the interplanetary medium. (There are probably also many more planetary satellites that have not been discovered). The first thing to notice is that the solar system is mostly empty space. The planets are very small compared to space between them.

The Sun is the richest source of electro-magnetic energy (mostly in the form of heat and light) in the solar system. The Sun's nearest known stellar neighbour is a red dwarf star called Proxima Centauri, at a distance of 4.3 light years away. The whole solar system, together with the local stars visible on a clear night, orbits the centre of our home galaxy, spiral disk of 200 billion stars we call the Milky Way. The nearest large galaxy is the Andromeda Galaxy. It is a spiral galaxy like the Milky Way but is 4 times as massive and is 2 million light years away. Our galaxy, one of billions of galaxies known, is travelling through the intergalactic space.

COMPOSITION:

The Sun contains 99.85% of all the matter in the Solar system. The planets, which condensed out of the same disk of material that formed the Sun, contain only 0.135% of the mass of the solar system.

Jupiter contains more than twice the matter of all the other planets combined. Satellites of the planets, comets, asteroids, meteoroids, and the interplanetary medium constitute the remaining 0.015%. The following table is a list of the mass distribution within our Solar System.

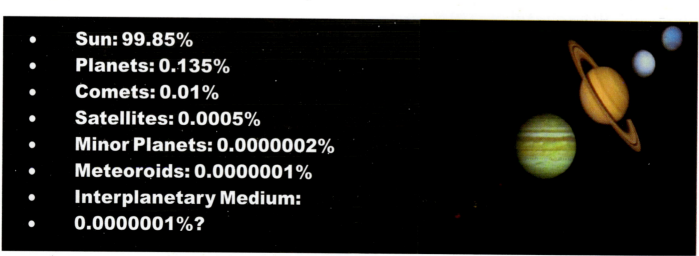

- Sun: 99.85%
- Planets: 0.135%
- Comets: 0.01%
- Satellites: 0.0005%
- Minor Planets: 0.0000002%
- Meteoroids: 0.0000001%
- Interplanetary Medium:
- 0.0000001%?

MERCURY

Planets and their Moons

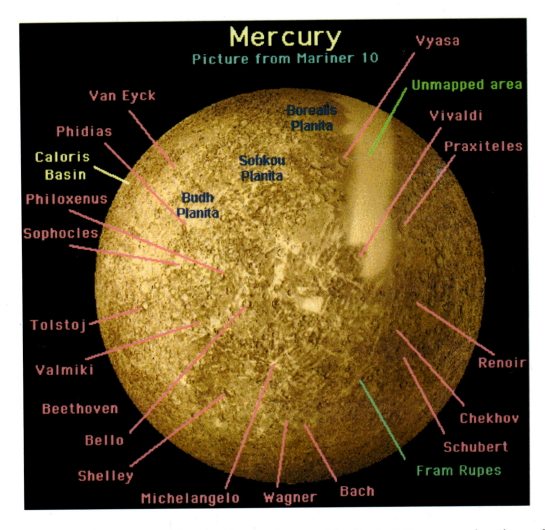

Scorched and blasted by the solar radiation, Mercury is the planet, closest to the Sun. This dry, rocky world has an atmosphere so thin that it barely exists. Of all the planets in the solar system, Mercury travels around the Sun fastest, but spins slowly on its axis. From the Earth, nothing is clearly visible on the planet surface, but our only close-up views date from 1970's when the space probe Mariner 10 was the first spacecraft to visit the Mercury.

The spacecraft flown to the Mercury three times and returned images and data of the planet) and revealed Mercury to be a heavily cratered world. All the astronomers are puzzled as to why this small planet has such a vast iron core.

The Mercury's Surface

The Mercury is very close to the Sun. So, it is difficult to observe it. Even a space based observatory, such as the Hubble Space telescope, cannot provide views of The Mercury's surface, since the Sun's rays would damage the telescope's sensitive instruments. With the aid of protective sunshields, the space probe Mariner 10 succeeded in producing detailed images of mercury. Its flight path allowed it to photograph only part of the surface, leaving more than half still to be explored. The Mercury turns slowly on its axis, taking nearly 59 Earth days to complete one rotation, but it speeds along on its path around the Sun, making one orbit in just 88 days. For an observer standing on The Mercury these two motions would produce an interval of 176 days between 1 sunrise and the next.

The Mercury turns slowly on its axis, taking nearly 59 Earth days to complete one rotation, but it speeds along on its path around the Sun, making one orbit in just 88 days. For an observer standing on Mercury these two motions would produce an interval of 176 days between 1 sunrise and the next.

MERCURY STATISTICS

Equatorial Radius (km)	2439.7
Distance from the Sun (km)	57,909,175
Rotational Period (days)	58.6462
Orbital Period (days)	87.969
Mean Surface Temperature	179°C
Maximum Surface Temperature	430°C
Minimum Surface Temperature	-173°C
Atmospheric Composition:-	
Helium	42%
Sodium	42%
Oxygen	15%
Other	1%

HUBBLE SPACE TELESCOPE

(HST)

Not since Galileo turned his telescope towards the heavens in 1610 has any event so changed our understanding of the universe as the deployment of the Hubble Space Telescope.

Hubble Space Telescope (HST) is a telescope in orbit around the Earth. Hubble orbits 600 Kilometers (375 miles) above Earth, working round-the-clock to unlock the secrets of the universe. Its position outside the Earth's atmosphere allows it to take sharp optical images of very faint objects, and since its launch in 1990, it has become one of the most important telescopes in the history of astronomy. It has been responsible for many ground-breaking observations and has helped astronomers achieve a better understanding of many fundamental problems in astrophysics. Hubble's Ultra Deep Field is the deepest (most sensitive) astronomical optical image ever taken. It uses excellent pointing precision, powerful optics, and state-of-the-art instruments to provide stunning views of the Universe that cannot be made using ground-based telescopes or other satellites.

Hubble was originally designed in the 1970s and launched in 1990. Thanks to on-orbit services calls by the Space Shuttle astronauts, Hubble continues to be a state-of-the-art space telescope.

THE VENUS

The Venus is called an interior planet because it orbits closer to the Sun than the Earth does, Venus is like a sphere of rock similar in size to the Earth but the comparison ends there. Venus is a dark, hostile world of volcanoes and suffocating atmosphere. Its average temperature is more than that of any other planet. From the Earth, we can see only the planet's top clouds. Hidden under this thick blanket of gas is a landscape moulded by volcanic eruptions.

  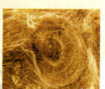 

VOLCANOES

Volcanic activity is evident all over the Venus. It's surface has long lava flows, volcanic craters, and dome-and-shield-shaped volcanoes. There are 156' large volcanoes that measure more than 100 km across, nearly 300 with diameters of between 20 and 100 km, and at least 500 clusters of smaller volcanoes.

Venusian Surface

Although the Venus is the closest planet to the Earth, its surface is perpetually hidden by clouds. Only in the last 30 years have scientists succeeded in seeing through its cloudy layers, using radar techniques similar to airport radar that can locate aircraft through cloud and fog. The data collected by Earthbased instruments and orbiting space probes have been combined to produce a global map of the planet. The most detailed data came from Magellan, the most recent and successful of all the orbiters. As this view of one side of the Venus shows, it is a planet of volcanic plains with some highland regions. Immediately above the Venusian surface is a clear region of atmosphere, stretching up to a height of 40 km or so. Above this is a thick, unbroken cloud layer rising further 20 km. The clouds, which contain dust and sulphuric acid, stop direct sunlight from reaching the surface, making the Venus permanently overcast. Finally, there is a clear, sparse layer of atmosphere stretching at least another 20km.

VENUS STATISTICS	
Equatorial Radius(km)	6,051.7
Distance from the Sun (km)	108,208,930
Rotational Period (days)	243.0187
Orbital Period (days)	224.701
Mean Surface Temperature	482°C
Atmospheric pressure (bars)	92

Atmospheric Composition:-	
Carbon dioxide	96%
Nitrogen	3%
Trace amounts of : Sulphur dioxide, water vapour, argon, helium, neon.	1%

THE EARTH

From the perspective we get on the Earth, our planet appears to be big and sturdy with an endless ocean of air. From the space, the astronauts often get the impression that the Earth is small with a thin, fragile layer of atmosphere. For a space traveller, the distinguishing Earth features are the blue waters, brown and green land masses and white clouds set against a black background. While travelling in the space, he can see many wonders of the universe.

In reality, all of us, are space travellers. Our spaceship is the planet Earth, travelling at the speed of 108,000 kilometres (67,000 miles) an hour.

The Earth is the 3rd planet from the Sun at a distance of about 150 million kilometres (93.2 million miles). It takes 365.256 days for the Earth to rotate around the Sun and 23.9345 hours for the Earth to move around its own axis. It has a diameter of 12,756 kilometers (7,973 miles), only a few hundred kilometers larger than that of Venus. Our atmosphere is composed of 78 percent nitrogen, 21 percent oxygen and 1 percent other constituents.

Earth is the only planet in the solar system known to harbour life. Our planet's rapid spin and molten nickel-iron core give rise to an extensive magnetic field, which, along with the atmosphere, shields us from nearly all of the harmful radiation coming from the Sun and other stars. Earth's atmosphere protects us from meteors, most of which burn up before they can strike the surface.

Besides affecting Earth's weather, solar activity gives rise to a dramatic visual phenomenon in our atmosphere. When charged particles from the solar wind become trapped in the Earth's magnetic field, they collide with air molecules above our planet's magnetic poles. These air molecules, then, begin to glow and are known as the auroras or the northern and southern lights.

EARTH STATISTICS

Equatorial Radius (km)	6,378.14
Distance from the Sun (km)	149,597,890
Rotational Period (hours)	24
Orbital Period (days)	365
Mean Surface Temperature	15°C
Atmospheric pressure (bars)	1.013
Atmospheric Composition:-	
Oxygen	21%
Nitrogen	78%
Other	1%

THE MOON

The Moon revolves around the Earth. It is natural satellite of the earth. The Moon is our nearest neighbour in space. It is about 3,84,000 km away. The Moon is a lifeless place. It has no air or water. There are tall mountains and flat plains on the Moon. There are also large round ditches called 'craters'. Some of the 'craters' are hundreds of kilometres wide. Many of them have been made by large rocks falling on the surface of the Moon. If you look at the Moon on a full moon night, you can see light and dark areas. The dark areas are plains and the light ones are mountains. Craters of the Moon can be easily seen with the telescope.

The Moon takes about one month to rotate. Since it revolves and rotates at the same speed, the same side of the Moon always faces us. The Moon shines as the brightest object in the night sky. But it does not give out its own light. It only reflects the light of the Sun to us. Therefore, depending on the position of the Sun, different areas of it reflect light to us on different days. That is why the Moon appears to change its shape everyday. The different shapes of the moon, as visible to us on the Earth, are called its phases. The gravity on the Moon is only about one-sixth of that on the Earth. This means that if you can jump 1 metre on the Earth, you can jump 6 metres on the Moon. Smaller gravity on the moon is the reason why there is no atmosphere on the moon. The Moon cannot pull the air particles with enough force. So, they escape into outer space.

THE MARS

The planet Mars was named after the Roman god of war because of its angry red appearance. Sometimes known as the red planet, it is composed of dense, rocky material and, along with the Mercury, the Venus and the Earth, it is one of the four terrestrial or like planets of the inner Solar System. The Mars is one and a half time more distant than the Earth from the Sun. In the late 1990's, the scientists began to study the red planet in unprecedented detail. They may yet uncover fossils, or even show that primitive life exists there.

Phobos and Deimos

Phobos and Deimos are the Moons of the Mars and were named after attendants of the Roman War-god Mars. Phobos is a dark body that appears to be composed of a type of surface materials, and it is similar to the type of asteroids that exist in the outer asteroid belt. Some scientists speculate that Phobos and Mars' other Moon, Deimos, are captured asteroids. However, other scientists point to evidence that contradicts this theory. Phobos shows striated patterns are probably cracks, caused by the pact event of the largest crater on the Moon whereas Deimos shows smoother appearance, caused by partial filling of some of its craters.

Deimos

Phobos

Temperature and Pressure

The average recorded temperature on the Mars is -63° C (-81° F) with a maximum temperature of 20° C (68° F) and a minimum of -140° C (-220° F). Barometric pressure varies at each landing site on a semiannual basis. Carbon dioxide, the major constituent of the atmosphere, freezes out to form an immense polar cap, alternately at each pole. The carbon dioxide forms a great cover of snow and, then, evaporates again with the coming of spring in each hemisphere. When the southern cap was largest, the mean daily pressure observed by Viking Lander 1 was as low as 6.8 millibars; at other times of the year it was as high as 9.0 millibars. The pressures at the Viking Lander 2 site were 7.3 and 10.8 millibars. In comparison, the average pressure of the Earth is 1000 millibars.

MARS STATISTICS

Equatorial Radius (km)	3,379.2
Distance from the Sun (km)	227,936,640
Rotational Period (hours)	24
Orbital Period (days)	686
Mean Surface Temperature	-63°C
Atmospheric pressure (bars)	0.007

Atmospheric Composition:-

Oxygen	2%
Nitrogen	3%
Carbon Dioxide	95%

THE JUPITER

The Jupiter is the fifth planet which is the largest one in the solar system. If the Jupiter were hollow, many Earths could fit inside. It also contains more matter than all of the other planets combined. It has a mass of 1.9×10^{27} kg and is 142,800 kilometres across the equator. The Jupiter possesses 63 known satellites, four of which - Callisto, Europa, Ganymede and Io - were observed by Galileo as long ago as 1610. Another 12 satellites have been recently discovered and given provisional designators until they are

officially confirmed and named. There is a ring system, but it is very faint and is totally invisible from the Earth. (The rings were discovered in 1979 by Voyager 1.) The atmosphere is very deep, perhaps comprising the whole

planet, and is somewhat like the Sun. It is composed mainly of hydrogen and helium, with small amounts of methane, ammonia, water vapor and other compounds. At great depths within the Jupiter, the pressure is so great that the hydrogen atoms are broken up and the electrons are freed so that the resulting atoms consist of bare protons. This produces a state in which the hydrogen becomes metallic. Colourful latitudinal bands, atmospheric clouds and storms illustrate the Jupiter's dynamic weather systems. The cloud patterns change within hours or days. The Great Red Spot is a complex storm moving in a counter-clockwise direction.

At the outer edge, material appears to rotate in four to six days; near the center, motions are small and nearly random in direction. An array of other smaller storms and eddies can be found through out the banded clouds. Auroral emissions, similar to Earth's northern lights, were observed in the polar regions of Jupiter. The auroral emissions appear to be related to material from Io that spirals along magnetic field lines to fall into Jupiter's atmosphere. Cloud-top lightning bolts, similar to super bolts in Earth's high atmosphere, were also observed.

MOONS OF JUPITER

Nearly four centuries ago Galileo Galilei turned his homemade telescope towards the sky and discovered four planetary bodies in orbit around Jupiter. These four satellites have come to be known as the Galilean satellites.

Over the course of the following centuries another 12 moons were discovered bringing the total to 16. Another 12 satellites have been recently discovered and given provisional designators until they are officially confirmed and named. Finally in 1979, the strangeness of these frozen new worlds was brought to light by the Voyager spacecrafts as they swept past the Jovian system. Again in 1996, the exploration of these worlds took a large step forward as the Galileo spacecraft began its long term mission of observing Jupiter and its moons.

Twelve of Jupiter's moons are relatively small and seem to have been captured than to have been formed in orbit around Jupiter. The four large Galilean moons; Io, Europa, Ganymede and Callisto, are believed to have formed the way Jupiter itself got formed.

JUPITER STATISTICS

Equatorial Radius (km)	71,492
Distance from the Sun (km)	778,412,020
Rotational Period (days)	0.41354
Orbital Period (days)	4332.71
Mean Cloud Temperature	-121°C
Atmospheric pressure (bars)	0.7

Atmospheric Composition:-

Hydrogen	90%
Helium	10%

Galileo Galilei
Astronomer and Physicist

1564 -1642

❝ I do not feel obliged to believe that the same god who has endowed us with sense, reason and intellect has intended us to forgo their use. ❞
— Galileo

Galileo Galilei was born on February 15, 1564 in Pisa, Italy. He was born to Vincenzo Galilei and Guilia Ammannati. Although he was a devout Catholic, Galileo fathered three children out of wedlock: two daughters and one son.

Galileo pioneered "experimental scientific method" and was the first to use a refracting telescope to make important astronomical discoveries. In 1609 Galileo learned of the invention of the telescope in Holland. That Galileo invented the Telescope is a popular misconception. From the barest description, he constructed a vastly superior model. Galileo made a series of profound discoveries using his new telescope, including the moons of the planet Jupiter and the phases of the planet Venus (similar to those of the Earth's moon).

As a Professor of astronomy at University of Pisa, Galileo was required to teach the accepted theory of his time that the Sun and all the planets revolved around the Earth. Later at University of Padua, he was exposed to a new theory, proposed by Nicolaus Copernicus, that the Earth and all the other planets revolved around the Sun. Galileo's observations with his new telescope convinced him of the truth of Copernicus's Sun-centered or heliocentric theory.

Galileo's support for the heliocentric theory got him into trouble with the Roman Catholic Church. In 1633 the Inquisition convicted him of heresy and forced him to recant (publicly withdraw) his support of Copernicus. They sentenced him to life imprisonment, but because of his advanced age allowed him to serve his term under house arrest at his villa outside of Florence, Italy. When he was under house arrest, he dedicated his time to one of his finest works, **Two New Sciences.** This book received high praise from both Sir Isaac Newton and Albert Einstein. As a result of this work, Galileo is often called, the "father of modern physics". Isaac Newton used one of Galileo's mathematical descriptions, "The Law of Inertia," as the foundation for his "First Law of Motion." Galileo died in 1642.

THE SATURN

The Saturn is the sixth planet which is the second largest in the solar system with an equatorial diameter of 119,300 kilometres. Much of what is known about the planet is due to the Voyager explorations in 1980-81. The Saturn is visibly flattened at the poles, a result of the very fast rotation of the planet on its axis. Its day is 10 hours, 39 minutes long, and it takes 29.5 Earth years to revolve about the Sun. The atmosphere is primarily composed of hydrogen with small amounts of helium and methane. The Saturn is the only planet less dense than water (about 30 percent less). In the unlikely event that a large enough ocean could be found, the Saturn would float in it. The Saturn's hazy yellow hue is marked by broad atmospheric banding similar to, but fainter than, that found on the Jupiter. The wind blows at high speeds on the Saturn. The strongest winds are found near the Equator. Here, the wind reaches velocities of 500 metres a second.

The velocity falls off uniformly at higher latitudes. The Saturn's ring system makes the planet one of the most beautiful objects in the solar system. The rings are split into a number of different parts, which include the bright A and B rings and a fainter C ring. The origin of these rings is obscure. It is thought that the rings may have been formed from larger Moons that were shattered by impacts of comets and meteoroids. The Saturn has 56 named satellites.

SATURN STATISTICS

Equatorial Radius (km)	60,268
Distance from the Sun (km)	1,426,725,400
Rotational Period (hours)	10.233
Orbital Period (years)	29.458
Mean Cloud Temperature	-125°C
Atmospheric Composition:-	
Hydrogen	97%
Helium	3%

THE URANUS

The Uranus is the seventh planet which is the third largest in the solar system. It was discovered by William Herschel, an amateur astronomer, in 1781. It has an equatorial diameter of 51,800 kilometres and orbits the Sun once every 84.01 Earth years. It has a mean distance from the Sun of 2.87 billion kilometers. It rotates about its axis once every 17 hours 14 minutes. The Uranus has at least 27 moons.

The two largest Moons, Titania and Oberon, were discovered by William Herschel in 1787. The atmosphere of the Uranus is composed of 83% hydrogen, 15% helium, 2% methane and small amounts of acetylene and other hydrocarbons. Methane in the upper atmosphere absorbs red light, giving Uranus its blue-green colour.

The atmosphere is arranged into clouds running at constant latitudes, similar to the orientation of the more vivid latitudinal bands seen on Jupiter and Saturn. Winds at mid-latitudes on Uranus blow in the direction of the planet's rotation. These winds blow at velocities of 40 to 160 metres per second (90 to 360 miles per hour). Radio science experiments found winds of about 100 metres per second blowing in the opposite direction at the equator.

URANUS STATISTICS

Equatorial radius (km)	25,559
Mean distance from the Sun	2,870,972,200
Rotational period (hours)	17.9
Orbital period (years)	84.01
Mean Cloud temperature	-193°C

Atmospheric Composition:-

Hydrogen	83%
Helium	15%
Methane	2%

THE NEPTUNE

The Neptune is the outermost planet of the gas giants. It has an equatorial diameter of 49,500 kilometres. If Neptune were hollow, it could contain many Earths. Neptune orbits the Sun every 165 years. It has 13 moons, six of which were found by Voyager. A day on Neptune is 16 hours and 6.7 minutes. Neptune was discovered on September 23, 1846 by Johann Gottfried Galle, of the Berlin Observatory, and Louis d'Arrest, an astronomy student, through mathematical predictions made by Urbain Jean Joseph Le Verrier.

The first two thirds of the Neptune is composed of a mixture of molten rock, water, liquid ammonia and methane. The outer third is a mixture of heated gases comprised of hydrogen, helium, water and methane. Methane gives Neptune its blue cloud colour. The Neptune is a dynamic planet with several large, dark spots reminiscent of Jupiter's hurricane-like storms. The largest spot, known as the Great Dark Spot, is about the size of the earth and is similar to the Great Red Spot on the Jupiter. Voyager revealed a small, irregularly shaped, eastward-moving cloud scooting around the Neptune every 16 hours or so. This scooter, as it has been dubbed, could be a plume rising above a deeper cloud deck.

Long bright clouds, similar to cirrus clouds on the Earth, were seen high in the Neptune's atmosphere. At low northern latitudes, Voyager captured images of cloud streaks casting their shadows on cloud decks below.

The strongest winds on any planet were measured on the Neptune. Most of the winds there blow westward, opposite to the rotation of the planet. Near the Great Dark Spot, winds blow up to 2,000 kilometres an hour.

NEPTUNE STATISTICS

Equatorial radius (km)	24,746
Mean distance from Sun	4,498,252,900
Rotational period (hours)	16.11
Orbital period (years)	164.79
Mean cloud Temperature	173°C

Atmospheric Composition:-

Hydrogen	85%
Helium	13%
Methane	2%

DWARF PLANETS

We now know that there are eight planets in our solar system recognized by International Astronomical Union, the authorized body to take such a decision on Astronomical matters. The IAU after demoting Pluto from the status of being a planet decided to create another category under the head of 'dwarf planets'. Under this category Pluto along with three other contenders of being called planet till yesterday are clubbed together. However, apart from these four, there could be number of bodies (Trans Neptunal Objects) which will qualify to be called dwarf planets. However, we will describe here four main bodies namely Pluto, Xena, Charon and Ceres.

New definition of Planet:- Celestial body in orbit around the Sun has sufficient mass for it's self-gravity to overcome rigid body forces so that it assumes a round shape, and has cleared the neighborhood around its orbit.

1. The Pluto

The Pluto enjoyed the status of planet of our solar system until August, 2006. It remained so for 76 years since its discovery in 1930. The Pluto is usually farther from the Sun than any of the eight planets; however, due to the eccentricity of its orbit, it is closer than Neptune for 20 years out of its 249 year orbit. Pluto crossed Neptune's orbit on January 21, 1979, made its closest approach on September 5, 1989, and it remained within the orbit of Neptune until February 11, 1999. This will not occur again until September 2226. The Pluto's rotation period is 6 days. By carefully measuring the brightness over time, it was possible to determine surface features. It was found that the Pluto has a highly reflective south polar cap, a dimmer north polar cap, and both bright and dark features in the equatorial region. The improved optics allow us to measure the Pluto's diameter as 2,275 kilometer. The Pluto's icy surface is 98% nitrogen. Methane and traces of carbon monoxide are also present. The colder than 70 Kelvin. The Pluto's temperature varies widely during the course of its orbit since its distance from the Sun varies due to its elliptical orbit.

Solid methane indicates that the Pluto is colder than 70 Kelvin. The Pluto's temperature varies widely during the course of its orbit since its distance from the Sun varies due to its elliptical orbit.

> **Cosmic Club loses member Pluto**
>
> The Pluto was officially labelled the ninth planet by the International Astronomical Union in 1930, the same body which took away its status on 24th August, 2006. The Pluto was named after Roman God of the under world. It was the first and only planet to be discovered by an American, Clyde W. Tombaugh. Venetia Burney gave Pluto its present name in her eleventh year. Little would have poor Pluto realized that the disturbances it causes in the Neptune orbit, which was how it made its presence felt, would be a reason for its losing the planetary status from the Solar System.

2. Charon

Charon was known as satellite of Pluto when it (Pluto) enjoyed the status of a full fledged planet. Charon's rotational period is six days same as that of Pluto. Pluto rotates synchronously with the orbit of Charon and so both are tidally locked resulting into continuously facing each other as they travel through the space. Charon's diameter is 1172

An artist's perception of Charon as seen from Pluto.

Km, just over half the size of Pluto. There average separation is 19640 Km, that is roughly 8 Pluto diameters.

> **Widow mourns Pluto's demotion**
>
> Clyde Tombaugh was 24 when he discovered Pluto while working at Lowell Observatory, Arizona in 1930. Tombaugh died in 1997 leaving behind his widow Patricia Tombaugh. Tombaugh had fought off other attempts to relegate Pluto but his widow said this time he probably would have endorsed the change, now that other planetary objects have been discovered in the Kuiper Belt, the belt of comets on the edge of the solar system where Pluto resides. "He was a scientist. He understood that they had had a real problem when they started finding several of these things flying around the place," Partricia Tombaugh said.

3. Eris (UB313)

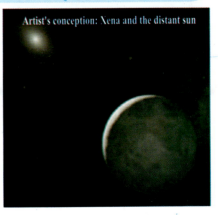
Artist's conception: Xena and the distant sun

The Eris was a strong contender for being the tenth planet before International Astronomical Union demoted the Pluto from the status of a Planet. Astronomers used the Hubble Space Telescope's sharp vision to measure the size of a large, icy object nicknamed Eris. They found that the Eris is slightly larger than the Pluto. The Eris is catalogued as UB313.

Its past nickname is taken from the lead fictional character in the 1995-2001 television series, "Xena: Warrior Princess."

Relative size

The Eris's diameter is 2,384 kilometres, about half the width of the United States. The Pluto's diameter is slightly smaller at 2,275 kilometres. This diameter may seem big, but it is actually two-thirds smaller than that of the

Hubble Spies Eris

Best image ever captured. The Hubble observations were not easy because the Eris is so far away. The icy world is 16 billion kilometers from the Sun, about three times as far from the Sun as Pluto. In fact, the Eris is the most distant object ever seen in the solar system. The Eris is so far away that it completes its journey around the Sun every 560 years. Its lengthy journey is more than twice as long as the Pluto's. Astronomers announced the Eris's discovery in 2005. They actually spied the object in 2003 while conducting a survey of the outer solar system at Palomar Observatory in California.

How bright is Eris?

The Eris is very bright. A bright object far from the Earth is either very large or very reflective, or a combination of the two. A large object appears bright because its wide surface area reflects lots of light. A smaller object also can appear bright if the material on its surface reflects most of the light that strikes it, like blinding sunlight from newly fallen snow.

Astronomers found that the Eris is very bright because it reflects lots of light. Its brightness is due possibly to frozen methane on its surface. The icy, rocky object may have had an atmosphere when it was closer to the Sun. As the Eris travelled farther away from the Sun, the material in its atmosphere froze and settled on its surface as frost. Another possibility is that the Eris's warmer interior is leaking methane gas. The gas freezes when it reaches the cold surface.

Where is the Kuiper Belt?

The Eris and the Pluto are the largest known bodies of the estimated 1,00,000 objects in the Kuiper Belt, a vast ring of ancient icy comets and larger bodies circling the Sun beyond the Neptune's orbit. Although the Eris is a small body, it is the largest object that has been discovered in our solar system since the Pluto's discovery 76 years ago.

But now the Eris and the Pluto both have been excluded from their planetary status and are simply known as Kuiper Belt Objects.

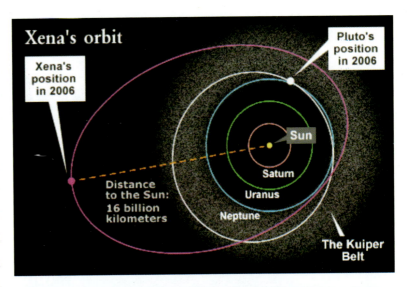

4. Ceres

The Ceres has got a diameter of 950 km. It was found by Italian Giuseppi Piazzi on 1 January, 1801. It got its name because Ceres, a goddess in Roman mythology, was associated with Sicily, where Piazzi was born. The Ceres orbit the Sun at a distance of 2.7 astronomical units, in the mainasteroid belt. Though it is the largest asteroid, Ceres is not the brightest because its surface is dark and reflects only 9 % of the sunlight falling on it. It only reaches 7th magnitude, so it is never bright enough to be seen by the naked eye.

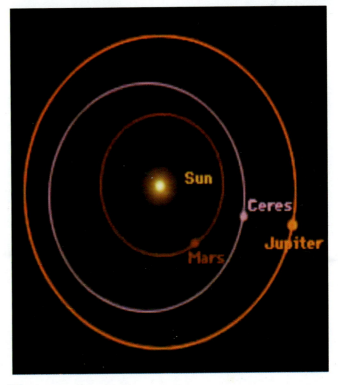

THE SPACE ODYSSEY

Have you ever realized how it feels to travel at the speed of 1 Lakh Km/hr. You guess, meanwhile I will take you on this exciting journey.

I am sure a rush of emotions full of anxiety, inquisitiveness and an adventurism comes to our mind at such a thought. But nothing of this sort happens to any one of us. Yes, if we consider our earth as a space ship, then, all of us are travelling at this speed when the Earth takes its majestic journey around the Sun. It keeps everything intact while it moves at such a high speed.

Have you ever wondered as to how every time we try to jump away from the earth, we fall back upon it. By now, you must have heard the famous observation by Isaac Newton of an apple falling on the ground and not going in Space. Of course, we all know that the fault lies with the Earth's gravity and there is nothing else to such a phenomenon. But is the Earth's gravity invincible? No, like all other things, the scientists have an answer to this problem also. If we can achieve a speed greater than 11x3600 Km/hr, we can escape into the Space. For achieving that kind of speed, we need Rockets. First time, it was Russian Scientist Konstantin Tsiolkovsky suggested in 1903 to use liquid fuel technology to power rockets which can go into the space.

GETTING IN SPACE

The most challenging task was to build a machine which could escape the scourge of the Earth's gravity. It was not a simple task to achieve. In fact, the fuel tank itself would be so large and heavy as to be unwieldy. The solution was found by inventing multi-stage rockets with different engines and fuel tanks. Each stage detached from the main machine after performing its task and thus making it lighter also. The next challenge lied in using the same vehicle repeatedly to bring economy to Space programmes.

500 years ago a Chinese Scientist Wan Hoo tried to go into the Space by tying rockets to his chair needless to say that he was never seen again. This speaks for Human hunger to fly in Space.

The first flight of the reusable space shuttle took place in 1981. It is made up of an orbiter with 3 main engines, external tank, and 2 solid rocket boosters. Cargo is carried in the orbiter's payload bay. Propellant for the main engines is supplied by the external tank. After each mission, the orbiter returns to the Earth, gliding or landing on a very long runway. The space shuttle launches satellites, space probes, space stations.

SPACE SHUTTLE

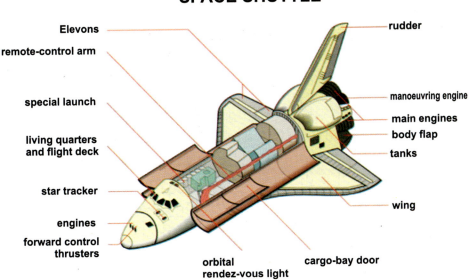

Breaking the Gravity Barrier

To escape the gravity of the Earth, we have to travel at an amazing speed of 11.2 km per second. The search for a vehicle which could reach such a speed ended with the discovery of Rockets. The earliest use of rockets is known when the Mongols used rockets against Arabs in 13th century. In terms of leaving the Earth, it was realized that solid rockets would not provide enough thrust to travel in space. The idea of reaching the Moon was given by 'Jules Verive' in his classic 1865 work 'From the Earth to the Moon' by launching 3 men and 2 dogs in space. But it was the Russians who developed the Liquid Fuel Powered Rockets which could overcome the force of gravity and go into Space.

American scientist Robert Goddard first used liquid fuel to fire a rocket, in 1926. At that time, people made fun of him when he suggested that this rocket could go up to the Moon.

Life in Space

It was dangerous to send human beings in space straight way.

Laika, the bitch, shown here in a harness, died from stress and overheating several hours after being launched into space.

The Scientists were not sure as to whether human beings can survive in Space. The Russians had already sent first artificial satellite in 1957. It was the safest bet to send animals into the Space. Who could have come handy than the best friend of the man, a dog. Russia launched the Sputnik-2 on November 3, 1957.

It was 5 times heavier than the earlier satellite and carried a dog as a passenger. The first animal to orbit the Earth was a Mongrel bitch called Laika. Unfortunately she died because of shortage of Oxygen as the scientist could not bring back the satellite on the Earth.

The Early Astronauts

Neil Armstrong

Uri Gagarin

Sally Ride

Valentina Tereshkova

After Second World War was over in 1945, there was a cold war between the USA & the, then, USSR. The USSR took early lead in space research. They were the first to send a human being into Space. Yuri Gagarin became the first human being to go into Space. His Space craft Vostock - took one orbit of the Earth in 1961. The Americans had to wait for one full month, when their fellow country man Alan Shepherd went into space.

In fact, the Americans were so cheesed off with this fact of the, then, Communist regime that they took a lot of pride by first landing their men on the Moon in 1969. Neil Armstrong of USA became the first human to land on the Moon. Valentina Tereskova, again a Russian, became first Woman to go into the Space in 1963. From the USA side, it was Sally ride (1983) who took this honour but not before another Russian woman, Svetlana Savitskaya had gone into the Space in 1982.

YOUR WORK-STATION
In Space

You want to have your work-station in space. You should not be claustrophobic because in Space, space is the greatest limitation.

Life on an early space craft was no better than being in hell. The astronauts were cramped in their capsules like gunny bags. Forget about toilets. There is a funny incident worth mentioning here. Alan Shepherd was stuck on a launch pad for hours because of some technical snag and he had to pee in his space suit. After this incident, astronauts were provided with large plastic bags to attend to their nature's call. Life in zero gravity is very difficult. We can get travel sickness in Space as we get it in a car, bus or ship. To make matter worse, if we throw up in Space, it will float.

DAILY ACTIVITIES

To be inside a space-craft is a big challenge. If somebody has phobia of small spaces, the space travel should be avoided, otherwise he will go crazy when trapped inside his capsule. You should be able to work upside down. The foremost requirement of going into the Space is to get used to zero gravity.

DINNER TIME

In early days of Space travel, food was paste sucked out of tubes like tooth pastes. The food which we take up is dehydrated. Before eating, add water & squeeze the plastic pouch around. Be careful that your dinner does not float. One has to be very careful of crumbly food as crumbs would float around like a dust storm.

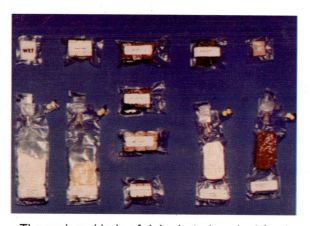

The various kinds of dehydrated packed food

Dinner Menu
Tea
Kidney beans
Mix vegetable
Chicken
Bread

Note : We can not serve crumbly food. The crumbs would float around like a dust storm.

TYPES OF FOOD

Preparation varies with the food type. Some foods can be eaten in their natural form, such as brownies and fruit. Other foods require adding water, such as macaroni and cheese or spaghetti. Of course, an oven is provided in the space shuttle and the space-station to heat foods to the proper temperature. There are no refrigerators in space, so space food must be stored and prepared properly to avoid spoilage, especially on longer missions.

Condiments are provided such as ketchup, mustard and mayonnaise. Salt and pepper are available but only in a liquid form. This is because astronauts can't sprinkle salt and pepper on their food in space. The salt and pepper would simply float away. There is a danger they could clog air vents, contaminate equipment or get stuck in an astronaut's eyes, mouth or nose.

Astronauts eat three meals a day - breakfast, lunch and dinner. Nutritionists ensure that the food they eat provides them with a balanced supply of vitamins and minerals. Calorie requirements differ for chicken, beef, seafood, candy, brownies, etc. Drinks range from coffee, tea, orange juice, fruit punches and lemonade. For instance, a small woman would require only about 1,900 calories a day, while a large man would require about 3,200 calories. There are also many types of foods an astronaut can choose from such as fruits, nuts, peanut, butter, chicken, beef, seafood, candy, brownies, etc.

KEEPING FIT

Our legs carry weight of our body and so is the other parts of our body muscles which keep on working while we are on the Earth partly because of our daily activities and partly because of Earth's gravity. But on board of a spacecraft, we have to exercise in space before going to bed. Floating around in space means we are not using our muscles and they become weak. Therefore, the space station is equipped with a gymnasium to keep our muscles fit & toned.

TAKE A BATH

Forget about your bath tub or your cold/hot shower which you are so used to on the Earth. Get ready for a bath in your work-station in Space. Water conservation is at its best in space. We use wet towel or a sponge bath. To clean our teeth, we either swallow the tooth paste or spit it in a towel. Going to loo, is very adventurous. First, we tie up ourselves with a belt and then, through a suction hose, we relieve ourselves. The faeces left behind is dehydrated and dried, till we reach back on the Earth and disposed off.

Using a special rinse-free shampoo on space shuttle discovery

SLEEPING IN SPACE

Sleeping accommodations aboard the shuttle vary depending on the requirements of the particular mission. The crew can sleep in their seats, in sleeping bags, in bunks, or by simply tethering themselves to the orbiter walls. The sleeping bags are cocoon-like restraints attached to the lockers where crew provisions are stored. In microgravity, there is no "up" and the astronauts can sleep as comfortably in the vertical position as the horizontal. For single crew shift missions (i.e. everyone in the crew shares the same sleep cycle / flight day), the sleep compartments are not normally aboard the shuttle. However, on dual crew shift missions (i.e. half the crew sleeps while the other half works), the sleep compartments are on-board to screen out the distractions of the working crew.

The two-level sleep compartment bunk bed provides sleeping space for four people. The first person sleeps on the top bunk, the second on the lower bunk. A third person sleeps on the underside of the lower bunk, actually facing the floor. A fourth person sleeps vertically in another bunk set against one end of the two-level bed. Bunks are more than 1.8 metres (6 feet) long and about .75 metres (30 inches) wide. Each bed is a padded board with a fireproof sleeping bag attached to it, and has perforations for ventilation. In Earth's gravity, your body sinks into a mattress, but because of the near weightlessness of space the hard bed board feels soft. Astronauts zip themselves inside the sleeping bags, leaving their arms outside. They snap together straps that circle the waist. Each sleeping compartment has a light for reading and side panels that can be shut for privacy. Eyeshades and earmuffs are available to reduce cabin light and noise. If all seven members of the Shuttle crew decide to sleep at one time, three more sleeping bags will be attached vertically to the bulkhead storage lockers. Two of the crew members must wear communications headgear so that they can receive calls from Mission Control or hear alarms.

THE EXPERIMENTS
IN SPACE

Shuttle and station astronauts perform many tasks as they orbit the Earth. The space shuttle is a versatile vehicle that provides facilities to perform science experiments, release and capture huge satellites and even assemble the International Space Station. However, the space shuttle was only designed to fly in space for about two and a half weeks at a time.

The space-station, on the other hand, is designed to be a permanent orbiting research facility. Its major purpose is to perform world-class science and research that only the microgravity environment can provide. The station crew spends their day, working on science experiments that require their input, as well as monitoring those that are controlled from the ground. They also take part in medical experiments to determine how well their bodies are adjusting to living with no gravity for long periods of time. Working on the space station also means ensuring the maintenance and health of the orbiting platform. Crew members are constantly checking support systems and cleaning filters, updating computer equipment - doing many of the things a homeowner must do to ensure their largest investment stays in good shape. Similarly, Mission Control constantly monitors the space station and sends messages each day through voice or e-mail with new instructions or plans to assist the crew members in their daily routine.

Before the International Space Station and the Russian Mir space station, the space shuttle was the only vehicle that NASA astronauts could live and work on for days at a time. The space shuttle would deliver satellites to space that could broadcast communications or peer into the edge of the universe. Of course, the crew members would carefully check all systems before finally releasing a satellite into Earth orbit. Probably the most famous satellite released from the space shuttle's payload bay is the Hubble Space Telescope. The shuttle has even returned to space three times with the new parts. After ground controllers are sure that the Hubble Space Telescope is in good condition, the robotic arm grabbing the satellite releases it back into space.

Research beneficial to life on Earth has been performed inside the space shuttle. For instance, protein crystals grown in space provide researchers insights into stronger, safer medications here on Earth. Plants grown in space help scientists learn how to grow healthier and stronger plants on Earth.

Plant experiments also help researchers understand the implications of feeding astronauts on long-term missions beyond low-Earth orbit. Studies have also been performed on astronauts themselves, mostly in an effort to determine the effects of microgravity on human bones and tissues.

SPACE WALK

Even though in normal course, when you are in Space we say that you are out in space. But actually you are protected from vagaries of space and its ambience by a well designed space craft. Suppose if we go down by a mile inside the ocean, we would be crushed by its sheer pressure. Similarly, when there is no atmospheric pressure, the molecules of a substance expands as much as possible.

Thus, if we step out of our space craft, our body will expand like a balloon till its bursts out. Secondly, there are enormous small pellets like structures which are floating around in space at a very high speed. Stepping out without precaution would be fatal.

We leave our spacecraft for repairing a satellite or testing a new equipment or for research purpose or to make International Space Station.

On Space Walk to repair the Hubble Space Telescope

Only six out of 157 NASA's Spacewalkers have been Female.

1. Kathryn Sullivan	1984
2. Kathryn Thornton	1992-93
3. Linda Godwin	1996
4. Tamara Jernigan	1999
5. Susan Helms	2001
6. Peggy Whitson	2002

Therefore, special space suits are provided to astronauts so that no harm comes to them when they leave their spacecraft for vacuum of space. This space suit protects them from changing temperatures, floating dust particles etc.

SPACE EXCURSION

You can go on a ten days Space Mission which will cost you about US $ 20 million and for an additional fee of about US $ 15 million, you can take a Spacewalk for 1.5 hours.

Yes, this is not fiction or day dreaming but an actual offer from a company based in VEINNA named Space Adventures Ltd. The company offers a ten days space mission costing US $ 20 Million. The package includes the mandatory six month training as an astronaut. What the company has come up with to attract outer space adrenaline junkies is a space walk option that will mean another six to eight days in space and an additional fee of US $ 15 Million. Clients who have spent initial US $ 20 Million will be passengers on the International Space Station (ISS) from where there space walk will mean unfettered freedom for 1.5 hrs. Space adventures offers many explore options-Orbital Space Flights, Commercial Lunar Missions, Zero Gravity and Jet Flights, cosmonaut Training, Space flight qualification programmes and reservations on future suborbital spacecrafts. All this has become possible with the setting up of permanent International Space Station. Believe me it has become like a taxi service. The shuttle goes up in the space and docks itself with the floating space station. Here it drops the new batch of tourists (Astronauts) and pick up the earlier batch so that they can be dropped back safely to the Earth and, then, the cycle begins. Of course, it is not so simple, as it sounds but we are very near to it.

The credit for being the first space tourist goes to Denis Tito. He was very adventurous. He took the strenuous journey when he was 60 years old. It cost him US $ 20 Million in 2001. That explains why he took this journey at such an advanced stage of life. You do not have that kind of money to spend at a young age. His vacation lasted for 8 days and he acted as a cook to astronauts. Another private company called The Space Island group has plans to build a space hotel and may be the next time, we will have discothèque, dancing there with some help, coming from lesser gravity.

INTERNATIONAL SPACE STATION

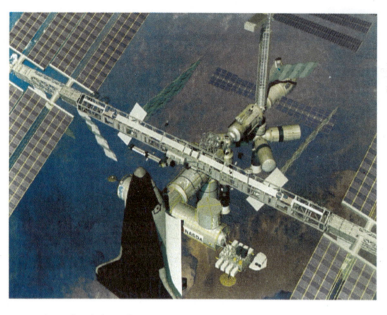

The US and Russia launched the first part of the ISS in 1998. Brazil, Canada, Japan and the European Space Agency have also contributed elements. The ISS carries a permanent crew starting with the arrival of the first 3-crew members in January 2000. The ISS is made up of more than 100 elements. The Biggest contribution including a connection node, solar panels, habitation module and 2 laboratories is from the USA. A core module, providing living quarters for the first few years, comes from Russia. Canada has provided a robot arm. Two connecting nodes originate in Europe. Most of the participating space agencies will help to transport supplies to the station.

MIR

On 20th February 1986, the United Soviet Socialist Republic launched the 3rd generation of Space Stations known as MIR (peace). Mir has been occupied by humans since early 1987 and by 1988 acted as a home for 2 cosmonauts for about an year. It has smashed every record in Space Station history including the longest stay in Space.

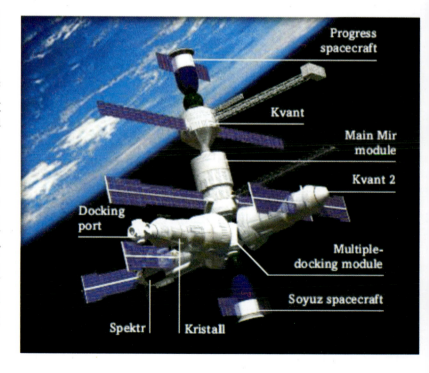

OUR MISSION

TO THE MOON & THE MARS

Missions to Moon

This is an image of the Moon taken by Star Tracker Camera B on Clementine orbit #110. It was taken on March 14, 1994. The Moon is illuminated entirely by the Sun's shine.

Since the first landing of American spacecraft Apollo II on the Moon carrying Neil Armstrong and Edwin Aldrin in 1969, the human imagination is running wild about having a colony at the Moon. Much of what we know about the Moon came from the Robotic Orbiters and Landers during the 1960s and 70s. Some scientists thought that spacecraft landing on the Moon would sink into its dusty surface. 12 men walked on the near side of the Moon between 1969 and 1972. They came back with nearly 400 kg of rocks and soil. On later missions, the astronauts drove around the Moon in a battery-powered rover. In recent years, the orbiters have shown that water ice may exist at the bottoms of the craters near the Lunar poles. Shaded from the Sun's rays, the ice may have been there for millions of years. This could be used for future explorers to make oxygen and water to drink. Europe's SMART-1 spacecraft is now orbiting the Moon.

MISSIONS TO THE MARS

A NASA artist's imagination of the Mars exploration rovers Spirit and Opportunity on the Red Planet

The Mars seems to be friendlier than the Moon for existence of life. The two powerful new Mars rovers have far greater mobility than the 1997 **Mars Pathfinder** rover. On June 10, 2003 the first Mars Exploration Rover (MER) spacecraft **Spirit** was launched on a Delta II rocket from Cape Canaveral, Florida. After a seven month flight, it entered the Martian atmosphere in January 2004. The rovers each had a spectacular landing, similar to that of the **Pathfinder** spacecraft. After entering the atmosphere, the rovers deployed their parachutes and airbags to land on the Martian surface. As of this writing, both rovers have revealed substantial evidence for liquid water at some time in the past at both the sites.

Opportunity found evidence of hematite, a mineral formed mostly in the presence of water, rock formations bearing chemical evidence of long-term water habitation, and physical evidence of water-formed rocks. *Spirit* had more difficulty, but eventually found evidence for water near Husband Hill, one of the hills named in honour of the lost *Columbia* astronauts.

Both *Spirit* and *Opportunity* have contributed a great deal of knowledge to our understanding of the Mars, with the rovers doing everything from geology to astronomy, snapping the first picture of the Earth from another planet. Much of the data has yet to be analyzed, and will surely yield even more discoveries.

FUTURE SPACE PLANES

VentureStar (X-33)

An ingenious wedge shape gives NASA's VentureStar, a distinctive look but also helps it to fly: It has a lifting body design. The X-33 takes off vertically but glides to a landing. Uncrewed flights within the atmosphere will help NASA decide whether to scale up the prototype.

X-34 Prototype

In 1999, the X-34 began testing the lightweight materials, thermal protection and landing systems needed for SSTO. It has small engines and is, therefore, launched in air with the help of a plane beneath it. The 21 test flight were planned to be extremely tough as X-34 travels 8 times faster than the speed of sound.

X-37 and X-38

Scientists are following the Venture Star and X-34 with designs for future space planes called X-37. NASA has laid down single most important rule for any designs that comes forward: the craft must be fully reusable. X-38 is the name given to a vehicle that could be used to return crew from the International Space Station.

— 39 —

X-43

The X-43 is an unmanned experimental hypersonic aircraft design with multiple planned scale variations meant to test different aspects of highly supersonic flight. X-43, is launched from a carrier plane. After the booster rocket brings the stack to the target speed and altitude, it is discarded, and the X-43 flies free using its own engine, a scramjet.

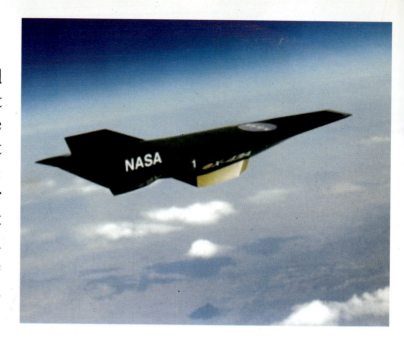

X-40A

The X-40A was an 80 per cent subscale version of the X-37 experimental autonomous spaceplane technology demonstrator, but lacking propulsion or thermal protection systems.

The X-40A flew seven approach and landing test flights at NASA Dryden in 2001 to reduce risk for the X-37 program, including in-flight evaluation of guidance, navigation and control software for its autonomous flight controls. Boeing built the X-40A originally for the Air Force as part of that service's Space Maneuver Vehicle program. It made one free flight in 1998 at Holloman Air Force Base in New Mexico before being loaned to NASA to aid the X-37 effort. The X-37 is being developed by Boeing for NASA to demonstrate advanced integrated technologies that would reduce the cost and risk of future reusable space launch vehicle systems.

INDIA IN THE WORLD

After India gained independence from the British occupation in 1947, Indian scientists and politicians recognized the potential of rocket technology in both defence applications, and for research and development. Recognizing that a country as demographically large as India would require its own independent space capabilities

In the early 1960's …India was slowly awakening to the Space age….Although rest of the world was preparing to reach the Moon…we were making our humble beginning…a small rocket took off from Thumba on the outskirts of Thiruvananthapuram, announcing the birth of the modern space age in India. That was when the Thumba Equatorial Rocket Launching Station (TERLS) formally came into existence. Over the years, TERLS have given birth to the Vikram Sarabhai Space Centre (VSSC) and to the Indian Space Research Organization (ISRO)…India was also aware of the fact that it would be better if it sent its own astronauts in space.

Keeping this in mind, India sent the, then, squadron leader Rakesh Sharma into space in collaboration with Soviet

Interkosmos space programme. He spent 8 days in space aboard the Salyut 7 space station. He was launched along with two other Soviet cosmonauts aboard Soyuz T-11 on the second of April, 1984.

> Rakesh Sharma, the pilot with Indian Air Force was the first Indian and 138th man to visit space. When asked by the, then, Prime Minister 'Indira Gandhi' how India looked from the space he replied "Saare Jahan Se Achcha", (Better than rest of the world). During the flight, Squadron Leader Sharma conducted multi-spectral photography of northern India in anticipation of the construction of hydroelectric power stations in the Himalayas. Salyut 7. Mr. Rakesh Sharma is now retired from Active employment.

— 41 —

INDIA ON THE MOON

India has announced its plans to explore the Moon and will send an unmanned probe there by 2008. The Indian Space Research Organization (ISRO) calls the moon flight project *'Chandrayan Pratham'*, which has been translated as *'Moonshot One'*. The 524.121 kg *Chandrayan-1* would be launched in 2007 or 2008, one of India's own Polar Satellite Launch Vehicle (PSLV) space rockets. At first, the satellite would circle the Earth, from there; it would fly on out into a polar orbit of the Moon some 60 miles above the surface.

The project's main objectives are high-resolution photography of the lunar surface using remote-sensing instruments sensitive to visible light, near-infrared light, and low-energy and high-energy X-rays. The European Space Agency (ESA) has agreed to support India's plan to send a probe to the Moon by providing three science instruments for Chandrayan-1. They will be identical to those already in orbit around the Moon on ESA's Smart 1 spacecraft, which is surveying chemical elements on the lunar surface. The Indian lunar satellite also would house a U.S. radar instrument designed to locate water ice.

The Haryana born American astronaut and space shuttle mission specialist Kalpana Chawla was one of the seven crew members who died aboard space shuttle Columbia which disintegrated upon re-entry into the Earth's atmosphere on 1st Feb, 2003. This was her second space mission the first being in 1997. Chawla was the first Indian born woman and second person of Indian origin to fly in space, following cosmonaut Rakesh Sharma who flew in 1984 in a Soviet spacecraft.

Sunita Williams was born on 19 September 1965 in Euclid, Ohio. She is a NASA astronaut. She is the second woman of Indian origin who has been selected by NASA for a space mission. Her roots go back to Ahmedabad in India. She had to prepare for T-38 flight training. She also worked in Moscow with the Russian Space Agency. Currently she is assigned to the Expedition 14 crew to the International Space Station and was launched on the Space Shuttle mission STS-116, aboard the shuttle Discovery on 10 December 2006 at 01:47 GMT.

SATELLITES OF INDIA

Aryabhata, the first Indian space satellite, was launched for India on April 19, 1975.

Later, Bhaskara-I, an Earth observation satellite, was launched for India on June 7, 1979. India launched its own satellite for the first time on July 18, 1980. It was the Rohini-1 satellite carried aloft on a Satellite Launch Vehicle (SLV) rocket from the Sriharikota Island launch site. Since then, India has invested a great deal of its space development work in complex applications satellites. The nation's two main interests are satellites for remote sensing and communications -- used for weather pictures, disaster warnings and feeds to 552 television and 164 radio stations on the ground.

Space organizations. A Space Science & Technology Centre (SSTC) was established in 1965 in Thumba. A Satellite Telecommunication Earth Station was erected in 1967 at Ahmedabad.

The Indian Space Research Organisation the (ISRO) was created on August 15, 1969, in the Department of Atomic Energy. Since then, the ISRO has managed India's space research and the uses of space for peaceful puroposes.

The government established the Space Commission and the Department of Space (DOS) in June 1972. The DOS conducts the nation's space activities for the ISRO at four space centres across the country.

The DOS reports directly to the Prime Minister. ISRO was placed under DOS on June 1, 1972, and made a government organisation on April 1, 1975.

TV satellite. By the end of 1985, the Rohini-3 communications satellite launched in August 1983 had extended nationwide television coverage from 20 percent to 70 percent of the population. Today it is about 90 percent. India's SROSS-1 satellite failed to achieve orbit when it rode the first developmental launch of an Augmented Satellite Launch Vehicle (ASLV) rocket on March 24, 1987. The second developmental launch of an ASLV in July 1988 also failed. Later, the third and fourth attempts were successful. In 1992, the Indian-built INSAT-2 geostationary communications and meteorological satellite superceded an American-built INSAT-1.

Geosynchronous satellites. One of India's Geosynchronous Satellite Launch Vehicle (GSLV) rockets was blasted off on April 18, 2001, from the Sriharikota Island launch site in the southern state of Andhra Pradesh on the east coast of the nation near the Bay of Bengal. It placed a 1.5-ton experimental communications satellite called GSAT-1 into geosynchronous orbit 22,300 miles above the Earth. GSAT-1 was a communication satellite with digital audio, data and video broadcasting using two S-band, one high power C-band and two indigenous C-bandtransponders. A GSLV rocket, similar in power to an American Delta rocket, can boost a large communications or weather satellite to a stationary orbit. India also plans to use GSLV rockets to send probes away from the Earth to explore the planets. Missions to Mercury, Venus and Mars are under consideration. India

would like to use the GSLV launcher to tap into the global commercial launcher market.

PSLV launches TES. India's Technology Experiment Satellite (TES) was launched on October 22, 2001,

aboard a Polar Satellite Launch Vehicle (PSLV-C3) from Sriharikota.The 2,440-lb. satellite tested new payload technologies, ranging from communications to remote sensing. It carried a panchromatic camera for Earth-imaging. PSLV-C3placed three satellite; India'sTES, Belgian PROBA and German BIRD into Polar sun synchronous orbit. October 22, 2001, aboard a Polar Satellite Launch Vehicle (PSLV-C3) from Sriharikota.The 2,440-lb. satellite tested new payload technologies, ranging from communications to remote sensing. It carried a panchromatic camera for Earth-imaging. PSLV-C3placed three satellite; India'sTES, Belgian PROBA and German BIRD into Polar sun synchronous orbit.
INSAT lofted by Ariane. The Indian National Satellite, INSAT-3C, designed and built by the Indian Space Research Organization (ISRO) was airlifted from Bangalore, India, to Cayenne Airport near Kourou, French Guyana in December 2001 in preparation for a launch on a European Space Agency Ariane-4 rocket on January 24, 2002.

INSAT-3C added much communications capacity to the INSAT fleet in orbit, including 24 C-band transponders, six extended C-band transponders, two S-band broadcast satellite service transponders and mobile satellite service transponders. The satellite beams commercial television signals to customers in India.

INSAT-3A launched in 2003.

An Ariane 5 rocket carried the Indian-built satellite INSAT-3A to space from Kourou on April 10, 2003. Insat 3A was built by the Indian Space Research Organization (ISRO) and carried a communication, weather imaging, and search-and-rescue payload. The 3,000-lb. satellite measured about 9 by 6.5 by 6 ft. Its solar panels spanned about 43 ft. On September 20, 2004 GSLV successfully placed EDUSAT. India also successfully placed on May 5, 2005 CRATOSTAT 1 and HAMSAT by PSLV C6. India also launched INSAT- 4A by Ariane from Kourou, French Guyana on December 22, 2005.

Heavyweight in Sky

This Indian spaceport is revving for a path breaking launch this year (2006) of the Insat-4C one of India's most advanced and the heaviest communication satellite. This 2,180 kg satellite, designed to enhance DTH television broadcast services, has been booked ahead of its launch by several Broadcasting Corporations. Insat-4C has been designed to last for a decade. As for the rocket that will cart this satellite into space the GSLV or the Geo-Synchronous Launch Vehicle the voyage in July, 2006 will be the first from the second launch pad built by ISRO at the cost of Rs. 400 crore. The satellite will be launched on July 10, 2006. This will be the first operational two-tonne class to be hoisted into Space from the Indian soil.

INSAT 4C launch unsuccessful

INSAT 4C, the most advanced communication satellite of India and the heaviest in its class, could not be launched as the GSLV carrying the satellite veered from its projected path 60 seconds after launch, and was self destructed over the Bay of Bengal. However, Indian Scientists are working overtime to launch another satellite as a replacement of INSAT 4C in near future.

Quick Facts

- At 2180 kg the Insat-4C is no lightweight. The last time GSLV lugged up a heavy satellite was in September 2004when the EDUSAT, weighing 1950 kg, was launched.
- Equipped with 12 high powered Kuband transponders, the spacecraft is designed to last 10 years.
- It is designed to enhance DTH television broadcast services and, ISRO, which is keen to ride the impending boom in the DTH services segment, sees big money here.

SPACE RECORDS
SOLAR SYSTEM

Brightest Planet

The planet that looks brightest as viewed from the Earth is the Venus. The Venus is the planet that approaches nearest to the Earth, but it is also the most effective at reflecting sunlight because it is covered by cloud. The Venus's cloud tops reflect 76% of the sunlight falling on them. When the Venus is at its brightest, it is at crescent phase. As the Venus's orbit is nearer the Sun than the Earth's, the disk of the Venus is only fully illuminated - or nearly so - when the Venus is on the opposite side of the Sun from the Earth, where it is at its greatest distance and smallest apparent diameter. When Venus is on the same side of the Sun as the Earth, only a crescent of its sunlit side is visible from the Earth, but that crescent has a much greater apparent area on the sky than 'full' Venus does at its much greater distance.

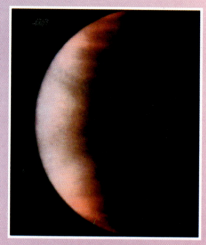

Hottest Planet

The surface temperature on Venus is between 460 and 480 deg C, making it the hottest planet in the solar system. The high Venusian temperature is due to the dense atmosphere of carbon dioxide. The atmosphere acts as an insulating blanket: the average temperature is 500 degrees higher than it would be without the atmosphere. Solar radiation penetrates Venus's clouds and its heat becomes trapped because of the properties of carbon dioxide, a phenomenon known as the greenhouse effect. In its early history, when the Sun was dimmer than it is now, Venus would have been cooler with oceans of liquid water. But over its first million years or so the water evaporated, contributing to the greenhouse effect, and was finally lost to space. As the temperature went up, more carbon dioxide was released from rocks on the surface leading to a 'runaway greenhouse effect' and the superheated state of Venus today.

The coldest object in the solar system

The lowest temperature ever recorded at the surface of a body in the solar system is the surface temperature of Neptune's Moon Triton, which Voyager 2 measured as -210 deg C, - 38 degrees above absolute zero. Temperatures on the Pluto are almost certainly very similar, though only ground-based estimates are available. They put the bright areas on the Pluto at about -233 deg C, with its darker areas around 20 degrees warmer. the Pluto and Triton seem to be very similar - more alike than any other pair of bodies in the solar system. The

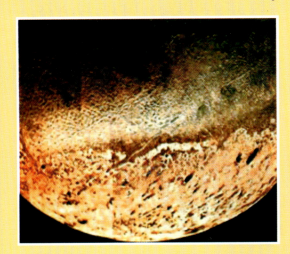

surface temperature of a Moon or planet depends on several

factors: its distance from the Sun, whether it has an internal source of heat, and the effects of any atmosphere. The Triton and the Pluto both receive very small amounts of heat from the Sun, have no internal heat, and are cooled further by the evaporation of ices from their surfaces.

Planet with most number of Moons

The Jupiter has the largest number of moons among all the eight planets of Solar system. It has in all 63 Moons. The four large Galilean Moons; Io, Europa, Ganymede and Callisto, are believed to have formed the way the Jupiter itself got formed. The Saturn comes second with 56 officially recognised and named moons.

The Uranus comes third with it's tally of 27 Moons. It is likely that all these three planets have more small Moons that have not yet been discovered. The origin of planetary Moons is not certain, but it seems likely that the larger Moons of the Saturn and the other giant planets, together with their small inner Moons, formed in place at about the same time as the parent planet, while the small outer Moons are asteroids captured at a later time.

Largest Moon

The Jupiter's Moon Ganymede with a diameter of 5150 km, is the largest in the solar system the Titan, the largest moon of the Saturn, is a close second. It was once thought to be larger than Ganymede. Third position goes to Ganymede's the Jupiter's Moon, Callisto. Both Ganymede and Callisto are larger than the planet Mercury (diameter 4878 km). Ganymede owes its status as the largest Moon to the thick mantle of ice that overlies its rocky interior.

The rocky cores of both Ganymede and Callisto are probably similar in size to

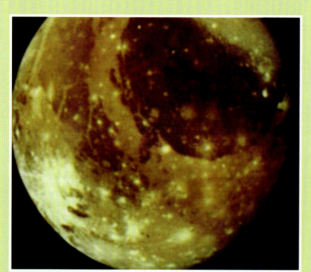

the two inner and smaller Galilean Moons of the Jupiter, Io (3,630 km) and Europa (3,138 km). However, due to their proximity to the Jupiter's warming influence, Io has no ice mantle and Europa has only a thin crust of ice, possibly with water or slush just below the surface. By contrast, the Ganymede's composition is about half ice and half rocky material.

Smallest Moon

The smallest Moon with dimensions that are accurately known is the Mars's satellite Deimos. Deimos is roughly ellipsoidal, measuring 15 by 12 by 11 km. A possible contender among other known objects is the Jupiter's Moon Leda, with an estimated diameter of order 10 km. It is difficult to determine with any accuracy the sizes of the small Moons orbiting the outer planets since most have been seen only as point-like images. The size estimate depends on the value adopted for the Moon's ability to reflect

sunlight. Deimos, and the Mars's other small Moon, Phobos, are both believed to be captured asteroids. They are both very dark and reflect only a few degrees of the light falling on them. They are similar to asteroids commonly found in the outer part of the asteroid belt and among the Jupiter's Trojan asteroids. The Leda is probably also an asteroid captured into orbit around the Jupiter.

Brightest asteroid

The asteroid that appears the brightest from the Earth is 4 Vesta. When it is at its nearest point to the Earth, Vesta reaches magnitude 6.5. In very dark sky conditions, it is just detectable to the naked eye. It is the only asteroid in principle visible to the naked eye. The next brightest, the largest asteroid Ceres, never exceeds magnitude 7.3. Though only three-fifths the size of Ceres, The Vesta is far more reflective. It reflects about 25% of the sunlight falling on it. The Vesta appears to be unique among the larger asteroids, with a

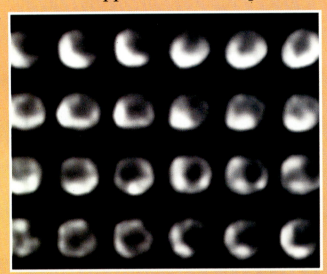

surface consisting of light coloured volcanic rocks, which account for its high reflectivity. The most reflective asteroids belong to a different class known as E-type (for enstatite). They are rare, and have reflectivities between 30 and 40%. The brightest of these asteroid is 44 Nysa, which reaches magnitude 9.7 though it is only 68 km across.

Darkest asteroid

The darkest of the larger asteroids - that is the one that reflects the least of the sunlight falling upon it is the Arethusa. Its reflectivity is put at 1.9%. It belongs to the C-type of asteroids, the C standing for 'carbonaceous'.

They are the most common type of asteroid and account for up to 80% of the population in the outer part of the asteroid belt. Other classes of dark asteroids are the P-type and D-type. The surfaces of all these objects are as dark as coal with reflectivities of around 2 to 6%. Other very dark asteroids among the larger members of the asteroid belt (with their reflectivities) include Atalante (2.4%), Hestia (2.8%), Aglaia (2.7%), Melete (2.6%), Cybele (2.2%) and Aurora (2.9%).

Largest lunar crater

The officially listed largest crater is Hertzsprung. It's diameter is 591 km and it lies on the farside of the Moon. So, it is permanently invisible from the Earth. It is a multi- ringed impact feature. Similar impact structures on the nearside of the Moon became flooded with lava which solidified into dark rock. These features are now named as maria (seas) rather than craters. Such volcanic flooding did not occur on the lunar farside.

As a result, there are many more very large impact structures on the farside that are described as 'craters' compared with the nearside structures. They include Apollo (537 km), Birkhoff (345 km), Korolev (437 km), Mendeleev (313 km), Planck (314 km) and Schroedinger (312 km). The largest crater on the nearside of the Moon is Bailly, diameter 287 km. The largest impact basin of any kind identified on the Moon is the South Pole-Aitken Basin, which is 2,500 km across and stretches almost a quarter the way round the Moon.

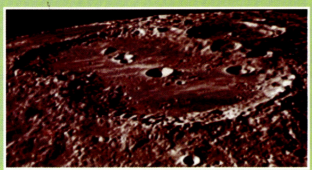

Highest volcano in the solar system

The highest volcanoes in the solar system are the Shield volcanoes on the Mars, The highest of all being is the Olympus Mons. Its summit is 26 km above the level of the surrounding plain, and it is nearly 500 km across. By comparison, the Hawaiian islands on the Earth rise about 9 km above the surrounding sea bed. Shield volcanoes grow in height gradually because repeated eruptions take place from one vent. The Shield volcanoes on the Mars are much larger than those on Earth for several reasons.

Though apparently no longer active, they probably formed early and remained active for a much longer time than the age of any volcanoes on the Earth. On the Earth, volcanic hotspots move as the continental plates gradually shift, so, volcanoes do not have time to build very high in a single place. In addition, the lower gravity on the Mars allows the erupted material to pile up much higher, before slumping down under its own weight.

COMETS

Comet observed over longest historical time

Observations of Halley's Comet, formally known as Comet 1P/Halley, have been traced back as far as 239 BC. There is no historical record for any other periodic comet that can be compared with that of the Halley's Comet. Halley's Comet uniquely has been observed at 30 apparitions over more than 2000 years because it is much larger and more active than other periodic comets. It was named for Edmund Halley who in 1705 realized the connection between several previous cometary apparitions, and predicted its return in 1758- 59. In 1986, the Giotto spacecraft succeeded in imaging its nucleus from a distance of only 10,000 km, and found it to be 15 km long by 8 km wide. The coma and tail, which

make the comet so conspicuous, form when heating by the Sun causes gas and dust to erupt as jets from the dark crust overlying the icy interior of the comet nucleus.

Brightest comet

It is not possible from records available to judge whether any particular comet can be considered the brightest. Since brilliant comets are greatly extended objects in the sky, putting a precise figure on their brightness is almost impossible. The impression gained of a comet is subjective and will depend on how long a tail it develops, and whether it is visible in a truly dark sky. The brightest comets of the 20th century have been the Great Daylight Comet of 1910, Halley's Comet at its 1910 apparition, Skjellerup-Maristany (1927), Bennett (1970), West (1976), Hale-Bopp (1997).

The brightest comets of the 19th century seem to have been the 'Great Comets' of 1811, 1861, and 1882. Earlier comets of special note for exceptional brilliance were recorded in 1743, 1577, 1471 and 1402. The closest and most brilliant return ever made by Halley's comet was in 837.

Closest approach of a comet to the Earth

The closest recorded encounter of a comet with the Earth was that of Comet Lexell in 1770. Its least distance from Earth was 0.015 astronomical units or 2.244 million km on 1st July 1770.

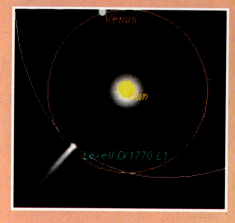

This is about six times the distance of the Moon. When at its closest, the apparent size of the comet was nearly five times the diameter of the full Moon. The comet was discovered by Charles Messier on 14th June 1770, but it was subsequently named after A. J. Lexell who studied the orbit of the comet and published his results in 1772 and 1779. He found that the comet had been projected

into its Earth- approaching orbit by a close encounter with the Jupiter 1767. Another even closer approach to Jupiter in 1779 once again perturbed the comet's orbit drastically, and it has been unobservable from the Earth since then.

Longest total solar eclipse

A total eclipse of the Sun occurs when the Moon passes directly between the Earth and the Sun, covering the Sun's disc completely. By a fluke of nature, the apparent sizes of the Sun and Moon in our sky are nearly the same, though both vary a little because the distances between the Earth and the Sun and the Earth and the Moon are not constant. This variation affects the duration of a total eclipse. In theory, the longest time totality can last during a total solar eclipse is 7 minutes and 31 seconds. In practice, no eclipse of such a long duration has been recorded. The longest of recent times was the eclipse of 20th June, 1955. Seen from the Philippine Islands, its totality lasted 7 minutes and 8 seconds. The longest eclipse predicted for the future is one on 5 July 2168, when totality will last 7 minutes 28 seconds.

Years with most eclipses

The maximum number of eclipses-lunar plus solar-possible in any calendar year is seven. The last calendar year in which seven eclipses took place was 1917 and the next such occurrence will be in 2094. In 1917, between 8th January and 14th December, there were three umbral eclipses of the Moon and four partial eclipses of the Sun, though one of those solar eclipses was very slight.

In 2094, there will be a penumbral eclipse of the Moon on 1st January, umbral lunar eclipses on 28th June and 21st December, partial solar eclipses on 13th June, 12th July and 7th December, and a total solar eclipse on 16th January 2094.

STARS

Largest Star

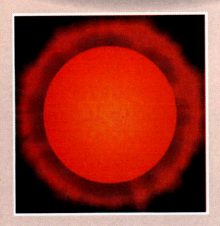

The largest star certainly belongs to the class of red supergiants, though the difficulty of measuring precise sizes for most stars means it is not possible to say for certain which is the largest. These stars as a group have radii which are comparable with the orbits of the Jupiter or the Saturn in the solar system - from 800 to 1,600 million kilometres, or between 1200 and 2400 times the size of the Sun. A possible candidate for the largest star is Alpha Herculis. Another very large red supergiant is Mu Cephei. Red supergiants are stars in a late stage of evolution. When the hydrogen fuelling the nuclear energy source at the star's centre begins to run out, a stage in the interior changes that take place causes the outer layers of the star to expand greatly. A red supergiant consists of a huge envelope of very tenuous gas around the central core of the star.

Hottest Star

The central stars of planetary nebulae are the hottest known stars. They have been detected with surface temperatures up to 250,000 K. One example of a planetary nebula with such a hot central star is NGC 2240. At such high temperatures, most of the radiation is emitted in the ultraviolet part of the spectrum, so the star is often not obvious in visual images of the nebula. Planetary nebulae form when evolved stars eject their outer layers. Their central stars are what were the stellar cores and their surface temperatures continues to rise after the nebulae have formed.

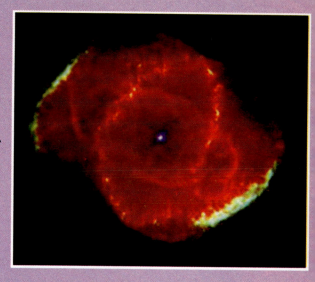

The maximum temperature reached is predetermined by the mass of the stellar core. Masses are thought to range between 0.55 and 1.2 times the Sun's mass. The greater the mass, the higher the maximum surface temperature achieved by the star.

Coolest Star

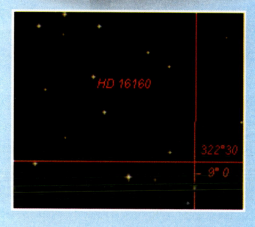

The coolest true stars are thought to have surface temperatures around 2,600 K. One example of such a star is Gliese 105C, imaged by the Hubble Space Telescope in 1995. The main factor determining a star's surface temperature is its mass. Theory puts the lower mass limit for a star at 8% the Sun's mass. Below this limit, it is impossible for the centre of a clump of gas contracting under gravity to heat up sufficiently for spontaneous nuclear fusion to start and maintain itself.

Potential stars that fail because their mass is below this limit are called brown dwarfs. Gliese 105C appears to be a true low-mass star, and not a brown dwarf. Its mass is put at 8-9% of the Sun's. Gliese 105C is the binary companion of larger star, Gliese 105A, also known as HD 16160.

Nearest Star

Proxima Centauri, at a distance of 4.25 light years, is the nearest star to the solar system. It seems to be linked into a loose triple system with the binary pair Alpha Centauri A and B, which are slightly further away, at a distance of 4.4 light years. The Sun lies in one of the spiral arms of the Galaxy-the Orion arm - about 28,000 light years from the galactic centre. In the Sun's

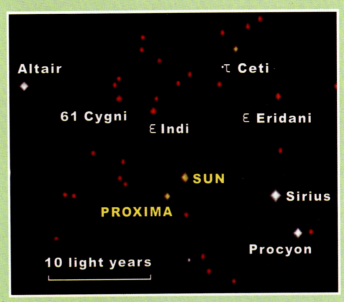

locality, stars are typically separated by several light years. The density of stars is lower in the gaps between the spiral arms and above or below the plane of the Galaxy. Close to the galactic centre, the stars are packed in much more tightly and are separated by distances of order one tenth of a light year.

Most Luminous Star

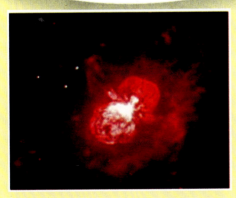

In 1997, astronomers using the Hubble Space Telescope (HST)) identified a star that could claim the record. They dubbed it the 'Pistol Star' from the shape of the nebula surrounding it. Though it releases up to 10 million times the power of the Sun, it is not visible to the naked eye since it lies 25,000 light years away, near the centre of the Milky Way, and is hidden by large clouds of dust.

HST detected its infrared radiation, which can penetrate the dust. However, a problem with identifying truly super luminous stars is determining whether candidates really are single stars or close multiple systems. Before the claim of the Pistol Star, Eta Carinae would have been the most serious contender, with an estimated luminosity 4 million times the Sun's. Following an outburst in the mid- nineteenth century when it became the second brightest star in the sky, it has now dimmed because it is surrounded by a cloud of ejected material, probably several times the Sun's mass.

Oldest Star

The oldest stars in the Galaxy almost certainly belong to globular clusters. It is suspected that all globular clusters are about the same age - around 10 or 11 billion years. By contrast the Sun formed relatively recently - about 5 billion years. There are several reasons for believing that globular clusters are very old. First, their more massive stars are all in advanced states of evolution, or have long since ended their lives as supernovae. Secondly, they are distributed throughout the spherical halo of the Galaxy, which suggests they are remnants of the era before the Galaxy collapsed to its present disc shape. Third, globular cluster stars contain very low proportions of chemical elements heavier than hydrogen or helium. This is because there were hardly any atoms of heavier elements in existence when these stars formed. The heavier elements have been created inside stars, then, recycled back into interstellar clouds to be incorporated in stars forming later, such as the Sun.

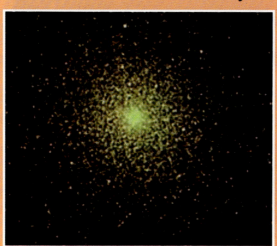

ASTRONOMY CHRONOLOGY

3000 BC **'STONE ASTRONOMY'** Stonehenge, built about this time in southern England, is a giant astronomical calendar with stones aligned to the Sun and possibly the Moon. Many other ancient sites are thought to have astronomical significance, such as the Egyptian pyramids and buildings in China and Central and South America.

380 BC **'EARTH CENTRED VIEW'**
A school is found by Greek Philosopher 'Plato' to 'thought' that will influence the next 2000 years. This promotes the idea that everything in the universe moves in harmony, and that the sun, moons, and planets move around the Earth in perfect circles.

164 BC **'HALLEY'S COMET'** The earliest recorded sighting of Halley's Comet was made by Babylonian astronomers. Their records of the comet's movement allow 20th century astronomers to predict accurately how the comet's orbit changes over the centuries.

750 BC **'LUNAR CYCLE'** In Babylon, astronomers discover 18.6 year cycle in the raising and setting of the Moon. From this, they create the first almanacs tables of movements of the Sun, Moon, and planets for use in astrology. In 6th century Greece, this knowledge is used to predict eclipses.

270 BC **'SUN CENTRED VIEW'**
Aristarchus of Samos proposes an alternative to the geocentric universe. His heliocentric model places the Sun at its centre with the Earth as just one planet orbiting around it. However, few people take the theory seriously if the Earth is moving through space, then why do the stars not move through the sky?

ASTRONOMY CHRONOLOGY

AD 150 'STAR CATALOGUE'

Ptolemy publishes his star catalogue, listing 48 constellations, and endorses the Earth centered universe. His views go unquestioned for the next 1,500 years, and are passed down to Arabic and medieval European astronomers in his book **'The Almagest'**.

AD 928 'ATROLABE'

The earliest surviving astrolabe is made by Islamic craftsmen. Astrolabes were the most advanced instruments of their times. The precise measurement of the positions of stars and planets allow Arab astronomers to compile the most detailed almanac and star atlases.

AD 1054 'SUPERNOVA'

Chinese astronomers record a sudden appearance of a bright star. Native American rock paintings also show the brilliant star close to the Moon. This star is the Crab supernova exploding.

AD 1543 'COPERNICAN SYSTEM'

A theory of Nicolaus Copernicus is published that proves that the Earth goes around the Sun, in contradiction of the Church's teachings. However he complicates his theory by retaining Plato's perfect circular orbits of the planets.

AD 1577 'TYCHO'S COMET'

Tycho Brahe observes a bright comet passing through the space, who proves that it is travelling beyond the Earth's atmosphere and there fore provides the first evidence that the sky can change its appearance.

AD 1608 'FIRST TELESCOPE'

'Hans Lippershey' a Dutch spectacle maker holds the record for the invention of the world's first refracting telescope. This invention spreads like wild fire throughout Europe, as scientists make their own instruments and their discoveries begin.

ASTRONOMY CHRONOLOGY

AD 1609 'KEPLER'S LAW'
Johannes Kepler publishes his New Astronomy. In this and later works, he announces his 3 laws of planetary motion, replacing the circular orbits of Plato with elliptical ones. Almanacs based on his laws prove to be highly accurate.

AD 1781 'Uranus'
Amateur astronomer William Hershel discovers the planet Uranus, although he, at first, mistakes it for a comet.

AD 1784 'MESSIER CATALOUGE'
Charles Messier publishes his catalogue of star clusters and nebulas. Messier draws up the list to prevent these objects, being identified as comets. However, it soon becomes standard reference for the study of star clusters and nebulas, and is still in use.

AD 1800 'INFRARED RADIATION'
William Hershel splits sunlight through a prism and, with a thermometer measures the energy given out by different colours; this is first study of star spectrum, discovering invisible infrared radiation and laying the foundations of spectrosocpy.

AD 1801 'ASTEROIDS'
Italian astronomer Giuseppe Piazzi discovers a planet orbiting between the Mars and the Jupiter and names it Ceres. William Herschel proves it to be a very small object calculating it to be only 320 km in diameter and not a planet. He proposes the name asteroid, and soon after similar bodies are being found. We all know now that Ceres is 950 km in diameter but too small to be a planet.

AD 1843 'SUNSPOT CYCLE'
German amateur astronomer Heinrich Schwabe who had been studying the sun for past 17 years announces his discovery of regular cycle of sunspot numbers the first clue to the Sun's internal structure.

ASTRONOMY CHRONOLOGY

AD 1845 'LARGE TELESCOPES'
Irish astronomer,the Earl of Rosse completes the world's first great telescope with a 180 cm mirror. He uses it to study and draw the structure of nebulas, and within a few months discovers the spiral structure of the whirlpool galaxy.

AD 1846 'NEPTUNE'
A new planet, called Neptune is identified by a German astronomer Johann Gotterfried Galle. He was searching in the position suggested by Urbain le Verrier. Le Verrier calculated the position and size of the planet from the effects of its gravitational pull on the orbit of Uranus. An English mathematician John Couch Adams also made similar calculations a year earlier.

AD 1895 'ROCKETS'
Konstantin Tsiolkovsky publishes his first article on the possibility of space flight. His greatest discovery is that, a rocket unlike other forms of propulsion, will work in a vacuum. He also outlines the principle of multi stage launch vehicle.

AD 1916 'BLACK HOLES'
German physicist Karl Schwarzschild uses Albert Einstein's theory of general relativity to lay the groundwork of black hole theory. He suggests that if any star collapses below a certain size, its gravity will be so strong that no form of radiation will escape from it.

AD 1923 'GALAXIES'
Edwin Hubble discovers a Cepheid variable star in the 'Andromeda Nebula' and proves that Andromeda and other nebulas are galaxies far beyond our own. By 1925 he produces a classification system of galaxies.

AD 1926 'ROCKETS'
Robert Goddard launches the first rocket powered by liquid fuel. He also demonstrates that a rocket can work in a vacuum. His later rockets break the sound barrier for the first time.

ASTRONOMY CHRONOLOGY

AD 1929 'HUBBLE'S LAW'

Edwin Hubble discovers that the universe is expanding and that the farther away a galaxy is, the faster it is moving away from us. Two years later Lemaître suggests that the expansion can be traced back to the 'Big Bang'.

AD 1930 'PLUTO'

Clyde Tombaugh discovers the planet Pluto at the Lowell Observatory in Flagstaffe, Arizona, USA. The planet is so faint and slow moving that the scientist has to compare photos taken several nights apart.

AD 1944 'V-2 ROCKET'

A team of German scientists led by Wernher von Braun develops the V-2, the first rocket powered ballistic missile. Scientists and engineers from Von Braun's team are captured at the end of WWII and drafted into Russian and American rocket programmes.

AD 1957 'SPACECRAFT'

Russia launches the first satellite, Sputnik 1, into orbit, beginning the Space Age. The USA launches its first satellite, Explorer 1, four months later.

AD 1961 'HUMANS IN SPACE'

Russia again takes the lead in the space race as Yuri Gagarin becomes the first person to orbit the Earth in April.

AD 1969 'APOLLO 11'

The USA wins the race for the Moon, as Neil Armstrong steps on the lunar surface on July 2oth July.

ASTRONOMY CHRONOLOGY

AD 1971 'SPACE STATIONS'
Russia launches its first space station, Salyut 1, into orbit. It is followed by a series of space stations. A permanent platform in orbit allows cosmonauts to carry out serious research.

AD 1975 'PLANETARY VISIT'
The Russian probe Venera 9 lands on the surface of Venus and sends back the first pictures of its surface. The first probe to land on another planet was Venera 7 in 1970, it had no camera.

AD 1977 'VOYAGERS'
NASA launches the 2 Voyager space probes to the outer planets. The Voyagers return scientific data and pictures from the Jupiter and the Saturn. Before leaving the solar system Voyager 2 became the first probe to visit Uranus and Neptune.

AD 1981 'SPACE SHUTTLE'
Columbia, the first of NASA's reusable space shuttles, makes its maiden flight.

AD 1990 'MAGELLAN'
The Magellan probe launched by NASA, arrives at Venus and sends 3 years of mapping with radar. Magellan is the first in a new wave of space probes including Galileo which arrived in the Jupiter in 1995 and Cassini.

AD 2002 'ESA LUNAR ORBITER'
The SMART-1 (Small Missions for Advanced Research in Technology 1) is a lunar orbiter designed to test spacecraft technologies for future missions such as a solar-powered on drive. It is to return data on the geology, morphology, topography, mineralogy, geochemistry, and exospheric environment of the Moon.

ASTRONOMY CHRONOLOGY

AD **2004** 'USA PLUTO FLY BY'
Work on this mission has been stopped for budgetary reasons. NASA is now seeking proposals for a new Pluto/Kuiper Belt Mission. It was originally scheduled for launch around 2001 and to arrive at the Pluto around 2013. The mission will consist of a pair of small, fast, relatively cheap spacecraft weighing less than 100 kilograms each. The spacecraft will pass within 15,000 kilometers of Pluto and Charon. They might include Russian Zoned probes designed to study the Plutonian atmosphere.

AD **2005** 'The 10th Planet!?'
Eris was a strong contender for being the tenth planet before the IAU (International Astronomical Union) demoted Pluto (KBO 134340) from the status of a planet. But now our Solar System is left with only 8 planets.

AD **2006** 'LOSS OF A FAMILY MEMBER'
The IAU (International Astronomical Union) demoted the Pluto from the status of planet and created another category called "dwarf planets" which will include the Pluto among others. Now there are only 8 planets in our solar system.

COSMOLOGY

The children and the young people of today will have to understand the relative value of the world environment in order to prepare for a better future life. The Dreamland's book 'The Race to Space' will provide them the basic knowledge about the whole Universe. First, let us establish what we know about this Universe. One, the Universe is infinite. Two, there are an infinite number of star systems. Three, there are an infinite number of planets surrounding these stars. Four, not every planet has life. Now, for a better understanding of the Universe, the children need to be familiar with the word Cosmology.

Cosmology is the study of the nature of the Universe and its beginning and ending. Until the 17th century, most people believed that everything beyond the Earth's surface was 'unknowable'. The breakthrough came when Kepler proved that the planets move around the Sun in elliptical orbits and Newton showed how Gravity explained why they moved as they did. These discoveries showed that 'Earth-based' laws of Geometry and Physics seem to work in space too.

At the beginning of the 20th century, the Universe was proved to contain countless galaxies in addition to our own. The Big Bang theory became generally accepted about 25 years ago. It says that the Universe began with a huge explosion, 10 to 20 billion years ago.

MILESTONES IN COSMOLOGY

1700s and 1800s : Astronomers contradict the simple explanation of Universe and show that stars are not distributed evenly throughout the Universe.

1916 : Albert Einstein publishes his general theory of relativity which brings about a rethink of space, time and gravity.

1920s : Edwin Hubble studies the speed of galaxies' motion. Using the Doppler effect he determines that all galaxies began moving away from one another 10 to 20 billion years ago.

1965 : Astronomers show that the Universe is full of weak radio waves.

1980 : Stephen Hawking's work supports the theory that the Universe began in a big bang. He also explains what happens when a star collapses and becomes a black hole.